Grace O'Malley

Michael Sheane

A.H. STOCKWELL
PUBLISHERS SINCE 1898

Published in 2023 by
Michael Sheane
in association with
Arthur H Stockwell Ltd
West Wing Studios
Unit 166, The Mall
Luton, Bedfordshire
ahstockwell.co.uk

Contents

Also from Michael Sheane

Ulster & Its Future After the Troubles (1977)
Ulster & The German Solution (1978)
Ulster & The British Connection (1979)
Ulster & The Lords of the North (1980)
Ulster & The Middle Ages (1982)
Ulster & St Patrick (1984)
The Twilight Pagans (1990)
Enemy of England (1991)
The Great Siege (2002)
Ulster in the Age of Saint Comgall of Bangor (2004)
Ulster Blood (2005)
King William's Victory (2006)
Ulster Stock (2007)
Famine in the Land of Ulster (2008)
Pre-Christian Ulster (2009)
The Glens of Antrim (2010)
Ulster Women – A Short History (2010)
The Invasion of Ulster (2010)
Ulster in the Viking Age (2011)
Ulster in the Eighteenth Century (2011)
Ulster in the History of Ireland (2012)
Rathlin Island (2013)
Saint Patrick's Missionary Journeys in Ireland (2015)
The Story of Carrickfergus (2015)
Ireland's Holy Places (2016)
The Conqueror of the North (2017)
The Story of Holywell Hospital: A Country Asylum (2018)
Patrick: A Saint for All Seasons (2019)
The Picts: The Painted People (2019)
Pictland: The Conversion to Christianity of a Pagan Race (2020)
Irish & Scottish Dalriada (2020)
The Roman Empire (2021)
The Ancient Picts of the Scottish Highlands of the Seventh Century (2021)
The Celtic Supernatural (2022)

Grace O'Malley

Grace O'Malley's Ireland

Grace O'Malley, better known in Ireland as Granuaile, was a pirate queen infesting the coast of Eirinn and further afield – even to Spain – in the reign of Queen Elizabeth I. For over 50 years she commanded fleets but she was also a trader. Powerful on land as well as the sea, she commanded her own army, leading it into battle. It was fitting that one day Queen Elizabeth and Grace would come face to face.

Grace was born around 1530 and her father was the chieftain of Umall, a small remote kingdom bordering Clew Bay on the coast of County Mayo. To strengthen his position, a chieftain often hired gallowglasses – Scots mercenary soldiers. Gaelic laws, known as the Brehon Laws, ruled over the Gaels and at the time of Grace's birth the English ruled only an area around Dublin known as the Pale. King Henry VIII's policy of surrender and re-grant of land took many years to take a hold on English ambitions to re-conquer Erinn.

In Grace's time much of Ireland was covered in forests and bogs; wild animals such as wolves, wild boar and deer roamed freely. There were few roads and even fewer bridges. It could take over a month to get from the west coast to the east coast, such were the state of the tracks. The country was famous for its cattle; the more cattle a chieftain possessed, the more powerful he was in the eyes of competing chieftains. There was little money and so barter was the means of exchange.

Kings like Grace's father lived in stone-built castles or towers, the ruins of which can still be seen; they were three of four storeys high surrounded by a defensive wall or bawn. The chieftain lived in the upper storey of the tower, the servants on the lower floor. The walls

1

of the castle were lime-washed and rushes were strewn on the bare flagstone floor for comfort. The followers of the chieftain lived in small round cottages made out of wattle, earth or stone and their cottages were clustered around the chieftain's castle for protection. There was little heat or light and even less furniture. The Gaels rose at sunrise and went to bed at sunset. In Grace's time the people enjoyed a varied diet; they ate fish, meat, vegetables and a type of porridge made from oatmeal and milk, flavoured with butter. They drank wine imported from both France and Spain and of course enjoyed a whiskey. Travelling musicians and storytellers entertained Grace; the harp and bagpipes were the most common instruments played. Such musicians also brought news and gossip to the countryside, for there was of course no postal service or newspapers back then. Chess, dice and cards were popular pastimes, and Grace gained a reputation as a shrewd gambler which earned her the nickname 'Grace of the Gamblers'.

For some years the Gaels of Ireland had feared a total domination of their island, for successive attempts to rule the Kingdom only ended in coastal settlements, otherwise the Gaels of Grace O'Malley's Ireland fought back at England by ships that were quite large – as large and seaworthy as the English fleets. Grace was a pirate, not a politician, but she was to make a few appearances at Elizabeth's court. In England, it was also the age of William Shakespeare, who was well received at the London playhouse.

Elizabeth did not like the Irish or Gaels, for the population was mainly Roman Catholic. Elizabeth was fiercely anti-Roman Catholic, for the Pope held the English Church in excommunication; her subjects were released from allegiance to her. Before the break with Rome, Ireland and England looked towards the Church of Rome for leadership in all matters; the popes loved their English subjects. Ulster was the main thorn in the side of the Anglican Queen. She had sent the Earl of Essex to subdue Hugh O'Neill who adopted English means of warfare. O'Neill was educated in England, but still the Gaels loved their 'Earl of Tyrone', as O'Neill had styled himself. He made an alliance with Spain, and Elizabeth feared that the Spanish

King would try to conquer England using an Irish base – though this never materialised through the centuries.

The Gaels hated the English, for they had been driven into the bad lands, and all the important posts in Ireland or Éire were filled with Protestants of the established Church. Also, Elizabeth had little love of the various Protestant sects: the Presbyterians and Methodists. Originally the kings of England were only lords of the country; it was left to Henry VIII to make himself King of Ireland. Roman Catholics were forced to worship in secret and Grace O'Malley was a Catholic sea queen. But the Gaels were not particularly a sea-going race, so Grace O'Malley was in a unique position.

The Irish were regarded as lacking any form of civilisation, and it was lucky that Grace O'Malley escaped her career without being executed. Grace was brought up in the Reformation years, but she took little part in the fights between the Protestants and Catholics in Ireland. Most of her career was spent in Munster in Southwest Ireland and not in Ulster; nor did she take any part in the O'Neill wars in the north of the country.

Born to the Sea

For hundreds of years the O'Malleys had been sailing their ships around the coast of Ireland and to far destinations, trading fish and plundering. Grace O'Malley's father Dubhdara commanded the fleet and was usually dressed in a linen shirt and tight-fitting stockings called trews, along with a leather jerkin.

During summer the herds of cattle were driven into the mountains to graze. More than anything else, Grace wanted to be at sea with her father. There was a story that Grace cut her hair and dressed in boy's clothes and stowed away on her father's ships. She would soon learn the ways of the sea and grow to become as good sailor as her father. She became an expert judge of the tides and the many moods of the sea; she became, as poets called her, a prophet of the weather. She learned about all aspects of sailing, of navigation by the stars and compass, and how to steer her ships around dangerous reefs. During the summer the O'Malleys fished for herring in the rich waters off Clare Island and Achill; the fish were then packed in wooden barrels and the herring transported to Spain by ships. The ships returned from Spain with cargoes of clothes, salt, wine, iron weapons and alum – a substance used for dying clothes such as cambric and damask – as well as Spanish fashions and furnishings for those who could afford them. Dubhdara had the biggest ships in Ireland, along with a number of galleys. Galleys were rowed by as many as 30 men, could hold up to 100 sailors and were fast and agile vessels in the water. The small boats were known as curraghs and coracles.

Wealthy merchants controlled the trade of Galway city, and the O'Malleys made the merchants pay taxes called tolls to sail through

O'Malley waters off the west coast. At this time there were no accurate maps of Ireland and the west coast, with its rocky headlands and underwater reefs, was much feared by foreign sea captains. Grace's father issued licences to Spanish and English fisherman to fish in the rich waters under his control off Clew Bay.

As Grace grew up she could see how important the sea was for the clan's income. Control of the sea made them independent: it was a lesson that she would never forget.

Grace O'Malley's First Marriage

When she was sixteen years of age Grace O'Malley's seafaring life came to an end. Her parents decided that it was now time for her to get married, but she could not choose her own husband. Her marriage was an important event for the whole clan because a marriage between two clans would protect the O'Malley clan in time of trouble. A suitable partner was sought for her among the ruling classes and Donal an Chogaidh was chosen. On her marriage, her father gave her a dowry consisting of a number of cattle and sheep, along with household linen and furnishings for their new home. Grace and her husband Donal lived in Bunowen Castle, which was on the coast. She and Donal had two sons and a daughter and everything boded well for the young Grace.

Donal was a reckless and warlike chieftain and he was at constant war with other clans. Grace assisted Donal in his attacks on ships sailing into Galway, taking tolls for safe passage. Soon the name of Grace O'Malley became feared along the coasts. The mayor and corporation complained about her to the English government in Dublin but there was little done to stop her.

This was the age of Elizabeth in England, daughter of Henry VIII, whose endeavours to re-conquer Ireland were soon to affect Donal and Grace. Later Elizabeth interfered in Ireland when she chose other potentates, a big set-back for Donal and Grace. Donal was now fighting with his neighbours over the ownership of his castle in Lough Corrib, known as Cock's Castle. The castle changed hands a number of times in the dispute but eventually Donal was killed in an attack by the Joyce clan. Grace was forced to defend the castle; the

Galway merchants sent an army to besiege her there and thought they had cornered the pirate queen at last. Food supplies in Grace's camp were running low and Grace had to devise a way of getting the soldiers away from the castle walls. She caused the Joyce clan to retreat but despite her success as a pirate, Grace could not become a chieftain in Donal's place because Gaelic laws did not allow women to become chieftains. Grace's sons, now young men, would have to wait their turn to put themselves forward for election as chieftain. Grace now returned to her home at Umhall in 1562 and some of Donal's clansmen – the O'Flaherty clan – followed her.

A Pirate Queen

Women could hold land in ancient Ireland and also own property. Grace had inherited land at Umhall from her mother. As her father was ageing, Grace took over control of the O'Malley fleet. She established a base on Clare Island situated at the mouth of Clew Bay; the castle gave her a clear view of it. It was situated in a secluded position, so that it could not be seen by enemy ships and therefore Grace could not be attacked.

From Donegal to Waterford, news of Grace O'Malley as a seafaring pirate grew. Many small kingdoms felt the brunt of her raids; in Dublin and London, stories about her reached the English Government who named her as the most notorious woman along the coast of Ireland. While other women looked after the home, Grace was busy leading her unfeminine life. Seafaring and plundering were in her blood; soon she had an army of 100 men. As a leader she had charisma and courage. She led her own men into battle, as a daring pirate. She was also ruthless when avenging a wrong done to her. During her time on Clare Island she bravely rescued a young man named Hugh de Lacy, whose ship had foundered on the rocks of Achill Island. She fell in love with Hugh, but he was murdered by the MacMahons, a neighbouring clan. After getting over his death she was intent upon revenge and when the MacMahons came on a pilgrimage to the holy island of Caher, near Clare Island, Grace swooped down like an eagle, capturing their boats and killing those responsible for Hugh's death. Now she sailed to Doona and took the MacMahon castle for herself.

Kidnapped

While returning from a trading expedition in 1575, Grace was forced to put in at Howth near Dublin which was then controlled by the English of the Pale. Here she paid a visit to the Lord of Howth, and when she knocked loudly on the castle door, a servant demanded to know what she wanted. She said that she wanted the owner's hospitality, and the servant said that Lord Howth was at his dinner and should not be disturbed. If Lord Howth had visited her in her castle in County Mayo she would have been obliged by Gaelic Law to give him food and shelter, but all she received at the castle was an insult.

Grace returned to her ships where she met a boy walking along the beach. She stopped to talk to him and found out that he was the grandson and heir of Lord Howth. Grace invited the boy on board the boat and set sail for Clew Bay. When news reached Lord Howth that his grandson had been kidnapped by a notorious pirate from the west of Ireland, he was greatly concerned and set out on horseback to make the difficult journey across Ireland, expecting to pay a ransom in gold and silver. Meanwhile Grace returned to Clare Island, taking care that her captive came to no harm. At length Lord Howth arrived in Umhall and begged Grace to name any ransom she wished for the safe return of his heir. She scorned his offer of gold and silver, which took the nobleman by surprise; she made him swear that the door of Howth Castle would never be closed. He decided to carry out Grace's wishes and gave her a ring to seal their bargain; the ring was kept in the O'Malley family for many generations.

Even into the present day, Grace's visit is remembered – many roads in Howth village bear her name in Irish: 'Granuuaile'. In the castle, which is owned by the current Lord Howth, her ransom demands are still carried out by the family: when the owner sits down to dinner, he has an extra place set at his table to honour the promise his ancestors made 400 years ago to Grace O'Malley.

A New Marriage

Events in Ireland would now affect Grace's life. In Europe the old Catholics and new Protestants were coming into conflict. Catholics looked to King Philip of Spain for protection and Protestants turned to Elizabeth of England. Elizabeth feared that Spain would use Ireland as a base to conquer their country, so if she wanted to continue to rule England, it was essential to control Ireland. It was proposed to send loyal Englishmen to Ireland to settle on Irish-owned land. With these settlers came English Judges, tax collectors and sheriffs.

Meanwhile Grace was looking for allies and found one in the person of one Richard-in-Iron; he was an ideal mate for Grace who was strong at sea. Richard Bourke had a number of castles on the north side of Clew Bay. It is thought that he got his nickname from the suit of old-fashioned armour he wore; but it is perhaps more likely that this name was acquired from the mine he owned on his island. In 1566 Grace and Richard were married, but after one year she divorced him (according to Gaelic Law she could leave her spouse after one year), locking him in his castle and installing herself therein, and anchoring her ships in his fine harbour. They then patched up their differences: even though Grace wore the trousers in her marriage to Richard, they made a good couple – he was powerful on land and Grace powerful on the seas, so that this made the English wary of crossing swords with them.

Toby of the Ships

In 1567 a son was born to Grace and Richard whom they named Tibóid – Theobald in English – who became known to history as Tibóid-na-Long – 'Toby of the Ships'. He was born on a ship during a violent storm.

But now Grace's ships were attacked by North African pirates known as 'corsairs', who were much feared by everyone. They often took women and children prisoners and bought them back to North Africa as slaves. These pirates had attacked many coastal villages, particularly on the south coast of Ireland. The corsairs managed to board Grace's galley and battle raged on deck. Grace was tired after the birth of her son and furious that her men could not beat off the corsairs without her; with sword in hand she attacked them with great fury: they retreated, leaving a number of their dead behind them. Tibóid was to become an accomplished seafarer; like his father, he was also skilled in warfare. When he was six years of age his parents fostered him with a neighbouring chieftain, for fostering was a Gaelic custom. It was considered a mark of honour to be the fosterer of the son of a great chieftain. It also bound clans closer together in times of peace and war. As a future chieftain, Tibóid was trained in warlike skills, in the use of the sword, lance, javelin and dart, both on foot and on horseback. Later as a youth he learned all about seafaring from his mother. Unlike others of his countrymen, Tibóid was able to write and speak in English and Irish and some of his letters are preserved in the English State Papers.

A Feminine Sea Captain

England continued to extend its rule into areas of Ireland that were then controlled by the Gaelic chieftains and lords. It was not long before it would affect Grace and her family. In 1571, Richard-in-Iron was elected Tánaiste – the heir to the ruling position – to succeed Shane Bourke, the MacWilliam (or chief) of Mayo. To become the MacWilliam was the ambition of every Bourke because the position bought great power, lands and wealth, so that Richard and Grace's future was bright.

In 1576 Queen Elizabeth's representative in Ireland, the Lord Deputy Sir Henry Sidney, marched into Connaught and summoned those that had not already appeared before him to do so in Galway. The MacWilliam and Richard-in Iron refused, for they did not like the idea of being ruled by the English. The Lord Deputy had only a small army to attack the MacWilliam and Richard so had to devise another means to make them submit. He bribed their gallowglasses – their mercenary soldiers from Scotland – away from them, so reducing the strength of their army. The MacWilliam feared that the English would attack him and so submitted to the Lord Deputy.

The MacWilliam promised that he would rule Mayo in future by English law and pay taxes to Queen Elizabeth. Grace heard about these events. She understood that, under English law, the MacWilliam's nearest male relation would now succeed him when he died, instead of Richard, his tanaiste. Her first husband had been deprived of his rights and Grace declared that this would not happen to her second husband. She decided to let the Lord Deputy see for himself that she and Richard were a force to be feared; if Richard

13

did not become the MacWilliam, the English would have a fight on their hands.

Sir Henry Sidney returned to Galway in 1575 and met Grace. He was impressed; she met Sidney with two hundred fighting men along with three galleys. He was aware that Grace was the most notorious woman in all the coasts of Ireland and realised that, with her large army and ships, she would make a better friend than an enemy. He also observed that Richard was playing second fiddle to his wife. The Lord Deputy had no ships of his own and asked Grace if she would bring her galley for a trip around Galway Bay so that he might examine the defences of the city from the sea. Grace agreed, but made Sidney pay his fare.

Imprisonment

Satisfied that she had made Sidney realise the extent of her power, Grace returned to her seafaring life. She sailed south to Munster to plunder the lands of the Earl of Desmond, the most powerful lord in Ireland. But things did not go according to plan: she and some of her men were captured. She was brought before the Earl at his great castle of Askeaton in County Limerick and thrown into one of dungeons where she was incarcerated for almost a year. Imprisonment was a terrible fate for Grace as she was used to the independence of the sea; she was now like a wild animal in a pen with the threat of death ever-present. Day after day she paced up and down in her small cell.

The Earl also had problems because the English wanted to get their hands on his lands to set up colonies. He was unsure what to do but thought Grace would provide him with the answer. So when the English President of Munster, William Drury, arrived with his army before the walls of Askeaton Castle, the Earl produced Grace as proof of his loyalty to the English crown. Drury was impressed and wrote to London about the notorious prisoner, accusing Grace of being the commander of thieves and a woman that competed with men. When he had completed his tour of Munster, Drury had Grace moved to Limerick jail. From there she was taken in chains to Dublin Castle, where important political prisoners were kept.

She had now been in prison for 18 months, accused of piracy, treason and plunder: execution was staring her in the face. Somehow she managed to obtain her freedom and in early 1579 she was released from prison; how she managed this remains a mystery. As rumours of the Earl of Desmond's intrigue with Spain increased, the English did not consider plundering the lands of a suspected traitor to be much of a crime any longer.

Siege

On her release from jail in Dublin Castle, Grace hurried back to Umhall and her family could not believe their eyes. They thought that she had been executed, because few prisoners ever got freed. There was much joy and celebration on her return but the news was not welcomed in other places. When the merchants of Galway heard of her release they feared that they might have to pay tolls again. They decided to stop Grace before she got started again. The merchants of Galway paid for an army to confront Grace, sailing into Clew Bay to lay siege to her castle at Carraigahowley. Grace was taken by surprise; she managed to hold out for 27 days before turning the tables on her enemies , chasing them out of Clew Bay and right back to Galway.

In November 1579 her former gaoler, the Earl of Desmond, finally rebelled against the English with a huge army, composed of many of his clients, lords and chieftains in Munster. The Queen proclaimed him a traitor: this meant that if he was captured or killed, his estates would be forfeited to the Crown. The English attacked his territory and the rebellion that lasted for four years had begun. He asked for help from the Connaught chieftains. Grace had no reason to help her former captor but her husband Richard–in–Iron set out from Munster with his army. Grace was furious with her husband; her only concern was to protect and provide for her family and followers. She also realised that her husband's action would serve to bring the English army out of her Umhall kingdom.

In 1580 the English governor of Connaught drove Richard and his forces from Munster through Galway back into Mayo. Burning

17

and looting everything in his path, his mercenaries deserted him and Richard headed back to Grace for help. Sir Richard Malby, the English governor, pursued Richard to the shores of Clew Bay but Richard was able to escape to one of the islands: Grace was left to deal with Malby. Grace opened negotiations with Malby; with much skill and cunning she at length achieved good terms and a pardon for her husband. More importantly she got the English out of Umhall.

The MacWilliam of Mayo

In November 1580 the MacWilliam of Mayo died. By Gaelic law, Richard should have succeeded him but the MacWilliam had accepted English Law so that his title and lands would instead be inherited by his next male heir: his brother. Grace and Richard joined their forces to fight for their rights. Grace's ships brought in mercenaries from Scotland and other clans in Mayo came out to support them. The English were still fighting the Earl of Desmond in Munster and their army was already stretched to its limit.

When the English realised that they stood little chance of opposing the couple in Connaught, they agreed to parley. Both sides met in Mayo and a deal was struck – Richard was to become the next MacWilliam, with lands amounting to seven thousand acres along with the castle. He was to receive all the payments which the MacWilliam usually received by Brehon custom (traditional Irish practice) from his client chiefs in Mayo. In return Richard agreed to rule his lands by English Law and to pay fifty cows to the English government in tax.

As the MacWilliam, Richard was knighted by the Queen and was now Sir Richard Bourke. The ceremony was carried out by the Governor of Connaught in Galway. Grace became Lady Bourke, as well as being Chieftain in her own right. But she was still known as 'Granuaile'. The couple were now at the height of their power: every clan in Mayo paid them homage as well as many dues in cattle, money, horses, sheep, produce and weapons, as was the Gaelic custom.

In April 1583 Richard died and Grace was once again a widow. She called together all of her followers and with her own herds – which numbered one thousand head of cattle and horses – she returned to Umhall. She settled in her husband's castle at Carraigahowley and soon she was back to the life she loved: the sea. She was now fifty years of age but fate had other things in store for her.

Sir Richard Bingham

Up until now the English had been excluded from Grace's lands, but she was still a powerful leader by land and sea. She had her own ships and army, great wealth in cattle and horses and of course her own stronghold. The arrival of Sir Richard Bingham as Governor of Connaught in 1584 spelt the beginning of the end, not only for Grace but for her beloved Gaelic world. When Spain sought Gaelic support in its efforts to have great influence in Ireland, Queen Elizabeth decided it was time to subdue the Gaels.

The fate of the once powerful Earl of Desmond was a warning to other Gaelic chieftains, for his great castle at Askeaton was gutted by fire and his lands burned and pillaged. For two years Desmond was hunted like a wild animal in the forests of Munster. When at last he was captured, his head was sent to Queen Elizabeth and his son was incarcerated in the Tower of London. By English law the Earl's estates were confiscated by the Crown and divided among the planters (English-speaking protestants) and soldiers who had fought against him. It was now the turn of Grace to lose her lands in accordance with English Law and Sir Richard Bingham was just the man to do it. Bingham was a military man, determined that the Gaels should be subdued by the sword … and very soon his aim became a reality. One of his first acts was to hang seventy people in Galway. He now attacked the Bourkes in Mayo and hanged the MacWilliam's tanaise, Edmund Bourke, and confiscated his lands.

The County Mayo chiefs rose up to protect their lands and property, but the Governor's brother seized Grace's eldest son and put him to death while he was in custody. Grace was devastated by his murder and vowed vengence on the English governor; her ships brought in more mercenaries or gallowglasses from Scotland to help the rebellion. Soon she was captured by Bingham, who trapped her near her castle. Bingham now executed two of her nephews who had been taken with her. Grace was once again in jail and Bingham was now intent upon making an example out of her. He ordered a new gallows to be built to hang her as a deterrent to others. She faced her fate with much courage, but her daughter's husband – Chieftain Achill – tricked Bingham into accepting him as a hostage in place of Grace.

Once free, Grace set sail for Scotland to hire more mercenaries. On her voyage north a violent storm overtook her ships; they were battered and broken and she was forced to put ashore in Ulster for repairs. Her family in Mayo were Grace's immediate concern, but she knew that if she returned to her home Bingham would be intent on executing her. She knew that there was little love lost between Bingham and the Lord Deputy, Sir John Perrot, so she travelled to Dublin to put her case before him. She asked Perrot for a pardon for herself and her family, who Bingham had accused of being rebels. Perrot agreed and said that he would do his best to take action against Bingham. By the time Grace got back to Mayo she found that the rebellion was over; the land was ruined and the Gaels were exhausted from fighting.

Perrot kept his word and Bingham transferred to Flanders. The whole of Connaught breathed a sigh of relief and hoped that they would never set eyes upon him again. Grace now returned to her beloved sea and made up for lost time.

The Great Armada

On 29th July the 138 ships of the Armada were sighted off the south coast of England. Great beacons were lit on the hilltops, conveying the terrible news across England. The long-feared Spanish invasion of England was now at hand. The English, however, were able to scatter some of the ships in the English Channel before they could land.

Luckily for the English there was a great storm that drove the Armada northwards towards Scotland and the English were saved. The Armada captains decided to return to Spain, but the wind blew with a vengeance along the north and west coasts of Ireland. The Spanish had no accurate maps of the region, causing many of the ships to crash on the rocky headlands, with some going aground on the rocky shallows. Thousands of Spanish sailors were drowned and those that managed to reach the shore were met with a mixed reception from the Gaels.

Few of the people in Ireland knew much about the Armada. As the great ships crashed on the rocks and split asunder, the Gaels only thought about the treasure that the ships possessed: had the Gaels helped the Spanish, the English would have reacted.

Many of the Spanish were killed or drowned and those that survived were stripped of their belongings and left to fend for themselves. Some of the Irish chiefs were helped by the Gaels like the O'Neills and the O'Rourkes in Ulster and got them safely back to Spain.

The English government feared that the Spaniards would join forces with the Gaels, especially with Grace O' Malley, and some of them did. The English made it a crime to help the Spaniards, punishable by death. Sir Richard Bingham was sent back to Connaught to put this order into effect and to round up the remaining survivors.

Bingham's New Forces

Bingham now sent an army to search the lands of Grace and her family; the army reached Grace's castle in February 1589 but the Gaels barred its path. In the battle that followed, many of Bingham's soldiers were killed. Grace and her followers rose in all-out rebellion to get rid of Bingham and soon the west of Ireland was up in arm. By sea Grace attacked the Aran Islands which had recently been given to an English planter.

The Lord Deputy came down from Dublin and invited Grace to a peace conference in Galway. Fearing a trap, the Gaelic chieftains refused to go to Galway and the negotiations took place outside the city walls. They demanded that Bingham should be removed from office. The chieftains were only biding their time and were waiting for the return of Grace, who had sailed to Scotland for more gallowglasses. The negotiations soon broke down and when seven of Grace's galleys full of mercenaries arrived in Erris in North County Mayo, the fighting resumed once again.

Bingham Fights Back

With the additional forces brought back by Grace, the Bourkes pressed home their advantage against the English. They recaptured Lough Mask, a Chief castle of the MacWilliam and plundered the county to the borders of Galway city. They decided to restore the ancient MacWilliam title, outlawed by the Crown and now the rebellion had an official figurehead.

Queen Elizabeth's patience had now run out: she ordered the Lord Deputy to find Sir Richard Bingham either guilty or not guilty of the charges brought against him by the Bourkes. Bingham was found not guilty and was allowed back to Connaught to bring the rebellion to an end by applying the sword. With a force of 1,000 he marched into Castlebar then set out against the Bourkes. The MacWilliam was injured and his followers rushed him away to Lough Conn. One of his legs had to be amputated and by Gaelic Law this misfortune prevented him remaining as the chief, so he resigned. Bingham pressed home the advantage and marched on Erris, killing and plundering as he went. The people fled before him into the mountains and the woods – the countryside was bereft of livestock and crops. He then doubled back to attack Grace.

Grace Knew Best

Grace and her men fled before Bingham to the safety of Clew Bay where, due to a lack of ships, Bingham was unable to pursue them. Instead he took his anger out on those that had been left behind; in his report to London he boasted that he killed many women and children. Grace could hear their cries and the sound of slaughter across the bay. The rebellion against the Crown now came to an end and Grace's men sued for peace. Bingham plundered her castle at Carraigahowley, stole her cattle and horses and lay waste to the countryside all around.

The sea and her ships were the only means by which Grace could provide for her family. She swooped down on the Aran Islands and plundered the property of the new English owners. Some of her relatives – including her son Murrough – were siding with Bingham and Grace was determined to teach them a lesson. Grace set sail for Ballinahich and attacked Murrough's castle of Dunowen. She ordered her men to burn and plunder the fortress and drive off the cattle. It was a severe lesson taught to her son and it worked, because Murrough never crossed his mother again.

Back to the Wall

By 1592 most of the main leaders of the rebellion had been killed in the war with Bingham. Like other chiefs in Connaught, Grace's priority was the caring for her lands and property and preserving the rights they had under the Brehon laws. If the Gaelic chiefs had united, they perhaps would have defeated the English but the chiefs often hated themselves as much as they hated the English. Ireland was still divided into many 'tuatha' or tribal regions. There were simply not enough new leaders to unite under a single banner.

An uneasy peace settled on Connaught. Although Bingham had robbed her of her cattle and other herds and had plundered her lands, Grace still had a number of ships. She knew, like her ancestors, that the sea was the best means to safeguard her position in Umhall. But there was another attack upon her, now led by her son Tibóid, putting her freedom and safety in jeopardy once more. Red Hugh O'Donnell of Donegal had escaped from Dublin Castle in 1591; to stop his father (Sir Hugh O'Donnell) rebelling against them, the English captured Red Hugh and threw him into prison, where he now started to plot with Spain against England. To prevent the English from finding out what was going on, he needed a diversion. In the spring of 1592 Red Hugh persuaded Grace's son Tibóid to attack Bingham in Connaught. O'Donnell promised Tibóid more than he could give, including help from Spain. On the strength of O'Donnell's promise, Tibóid started a rebellion in County Mayo and attacked Bingham at Cloonagashel Castle. The assault was unsuccessful and Tibóid's army retreated: O'Donnell had failed to deliver on his promise of help.

Bingham was furious and wanted revenge and came with a force into Tibóid's territory of Burrishoole, near Grace's home. The countryside was again stripped of its wealth and fires burned. English warships sailed into Grace's kingdom at Clew Bay and captured her fleet. For the first time the secrets of Grace's sea empire were revealed; the maze of islands, channels, hidden reefs, shallows and harbours that had protected her for many years had now been uncovered by the English. No longer could she run before the wind on missions of trade and plunder, or bring in mercenaries from Scotland.

A Letter to Queen Elizabeth

Bingham was well pleased with the success of his mission against Grace, who had been the major obstacle to his efforts in Connaught. He wrote to the English court boasting how he had attacked Grace's territory, making her powerless; but Grace did not take this lying down. She hated Bingham.

Grace was now 63 but her lands had been devastated and her people left starving. English warships patrolled the coast of her domain, but she was now plotting her next move and what a crafty move this was to be.

Bingham was master of Mayo and to get rid of him she wrote her first letter to Queen Elizabeth in the spring of 1593. Aware that Bingham had already blackened her name at court, Grace went ahead and presented her case to Elizabeth. She chose her words carefully, influencing the secretary of state Lord Burghley. She told Elizabeth that it was Bingham's harsh treatment of her and her family that had forced her to rise up in rebellion. She was also aware under English law that her lands could be confiscated. She realised that the only way to achieve this was to ask Elizabeth not to confiscate her lands. In the guise of fighting for the Queen, she could therefore get the better of Bingham, so continuing her life at sea.

She also asked for compensation for the damage done to her land and for the fortune in horses and cattle that Bingham had stolen from her. Elizabeth and Grace were of the same age and Grace played for the sympathy vote and asked the Queen to take into consideration her great age and the little time that she had left to live. While the letter made its way to the English court something happened that added new urgency to her pleas, which made Grace embark on the most dangerous voyage of her life.

The Plan

The English now knocked on the doors of Ulster, the last stronghold of Gaelic power in Ireland. They were confident of subduing the north after their victory in Connaught. Fearing that the English would overrun Ulster, O'Neill of Tyrone and O'Donnell of Donegal agreed to sink their differences and hold out against the English Crown. They wrote to the King of Spain to seek help against the English. Now the English moved against Ulster; the whole of Monaghan was declared Crown property and its chieftain was executed. They next moved against Maguire of Fermanagh, while Bingham looted and burned the Lordship of Breffni. During the attack on O'Rourke, Bingham claimed that he had intercepted a letter from Grace's son Tibóid implicating him in a plot to raise a new rebellion in County Mayo. Bingham had hoped to get rid of him and Grace swung into action to save her son's life; she again approached Elizabeth. If Grace landed on English soil she was aware that she might be thrown into the Tower and executed. She asked the Earl of Ormond to introduce her to the Queen, so that in June 1593 Grace set sail from Clew Bay on the most important voyage of her life.

Into the Lion's Den

Bingham reminded Elizabeth of all the trouble Grace had caused the Crown over the last 40 years. On board Grace's ships were some of her relations. The river Thames teamed with ships, for London was one of the busiest ports in the world. Along the banks of the Thames she saw the rotting corpses of pirates who had troubled Elizabeth. London was full of narrow streets bordered by houses, shops and taverns. Contacting Elizabeth would take longer than she anticipated.

A Lot of Questions

Grace did not obtain an interview with Elizabeth immediately. The Queen's secretary Lord Burghley had read the letter Grace had sent to Elizabeth; he sent Grace a list of 18 questions ranging from questions about her mother, father and children to questions of law and customs of Ireland in relation to women, their dowries and inheritance. Grace would have to be careful how she answered these questions: if she answered falsely she might never see the Queen and her son would die. She gave him an account of her life up to the death of her husband Richard. She mentioned how Bingham had stolen her cattle, lands and castles.

In July 1593 she received news that the Queen would see her at her palace of Greenwich.

Good Queen Bess

Elizabeth was much liked by her subjects and by 1593 she had been on the throne for 35 years. Poets wrote songs about her and it was the age of Shakespeare. The Queen never married. She could speak and write many languages including Latin. She had much physical energy and although there was much feasting at court she ate and drank modestly. She was tight-fisted about money. She was a great dresser and wore magnificent gowns. She had a hot temper. She boxed the ears of nobles when they displeased her. She had a razor-sharp tongue, Grace and Elizabeth were in many respects birds of a feather, being powerful women in what was mainly a man's world.

Her Meeting with the Queen

In July 1593, Grace's galley tied up near Greenwich Palace. Grace and her followers were led through the long corridors of the palace, past large rooms, stairs and galleries with high ceilings decorated with intricate plasterwork. It was a far cry from the living conditions in her stone castle at Carraighowley. When she left Greenwich it would either be as a captive or as a free woman. To the save the life of her son she would have to convince the Queen to go against the advice of her own governor. They now approached Elizabeth's private chamber. She looked at Grace with awe, at this old woman who had been through so much.

The court had also heard about Sir Philip Sidney, commander of rebels and pirates, the scourge of English merchant ships. As the doors of the Queen's chamber closed Grace was aware that Elizabeth might have her executed along with her son. The Queen was dressed in a richly embroidered gown studded with diamonds and precious gems which shone in the sunlight. Her face was covered in powder and rouge. Her teeth were black and her head was covered in a red wig. Grace, on the other hand, had a bare face, no powder. Elizabeth realised that she was in the presence of someone special.

Grace did not need powder or fine dresses to mark her out as a leader. Elizabeth was High Admiral of her Navy and chief commander of her armies while Grace was a pirate queen. Unlike Grace, Elizabeth had never led her troops into battle or sailed downriver at Greenwich. It was said that the two women spoke to each other in Latin, because Grace could only speak a little English though she knew a little Spanish. Elizabeth asked Grace questions about her rebellions against the Crown and if it was true that she had marched against her own son. Grace explained that Connaught was in a sorry state where the land had been devastated, led by Bingham; instead of justice, Bingham had brought only grief to her and her people. The Queen listened with pity to Grace's story. Grace asked if her son could be released from prison and Elizabeth said that in the meantime her son would be treated well: in Bingham's custody.

Now Grace was ready to play her trump card: she had to get Bingham off her back. She asked Elizabeth if she could return to her seafaring ways and the Queen agreed. Grace had pulled a fast one and could now return to her former trade by sea, this time with Elizabeth's permission. There was nothing that Bingham could do to stop her. The Queen wrote to a letter to Bingham. She ordered Bingham to release her son along with his half-brother to live in peace and enjoy life with Grace in her old age. Grace took her leave of the Queen and her court, her mission a success. So impressed was she by Grace that the Queen, when drawing up a new map of Ireland, ordered that Grace's name be included as chieftain of Mayo. She was the only woman whose name had ever appeared on a map of a country. Armed with Elizabeth's letter, Grace set sail for Ireland to arrive in Clew Bay in September.

Bingham's Revenge

Upon her return to Mayo, Grace confronted Bingham with Queen Elizabeth's letter, demanded the immediate release of her son and the return of her ships. Bingham was furious; he realised that she had pulled the wool over the Queen's eyes. She had played the part of the 'wronged woman' at court, which meant that Grace could now pursue her plundering activities while still being loyal to the Queen.

Bingham realised the trouble that Grace could still be causing so he ignored the Queen's orders as long as he dared. Grace threatened that she would return to court and inform the Queen, and Bingham – much against his better judgement – agreed to her terms, releasing Tibóid in November. Her son had been tortured in prison and could hardly stand, despite the Queen's promises that he would come to no harm.

At Tibóid's release, Grace prepared to build more galleys but Bingham vowed to stop her. Just as her galleys were ready to set sail in the spring of 1594, he pounced. He stationed his troops at Grace's castle and ordered them to accompany her ships when on plundering. Grace now realised that the game was up, with English ships tailing her.

Bingham was still the master of much of Mayo. Soon food began to run out, as Bingham's men plundered Clew Bay, leaving it bare. Grace was now faced with starvation: she knew that she must take action. In March 1595, under cover of darkness, with her family and crew, her galley stole out of Clew Bay and headed south sailing along the Munster coast until she reached Carrick-on-Suit, home of the Earl of Ormond. With the Earl's help she wrote once again to the

Queen's secretary, Lord Burghley – she said that Bingham had plans to kill her. It was her intention to go straight to London, but political events intervened.

The Showdown

In the summer of 1595 Hugh O'Neill, Earl of Tyrone, and O'Donnell of Donegal went into open rebellion against the Crown, hoping to establish an independent state in the north of Ireland. Bingham was removed as Governor of Connaught and was sent to prison. It was not long until Grace was back on her sea, her ships being sighted off the coast of Clare. In 1596 at the age of 66, Grace sailed to Scotland as a result of attacks from there to her lands in Count Mayo. Red Hugh O'Donnell raided Mayo, which forced Grace to change sides from O'Donnell to the English. There were also inter-tribal wars that weakened the Gaelic position of Grace and the O'Neills of Tyrone. O'Donnell hit back, capturing Tibóid and raiding his lands around Clew Bay. Grace was powerless to stop him. Famine stalked Mayo and the people were on the verge of starvation. Grace and Tibóid were forced to live on board their ships. In August 1597 Grace and her followers came to terms with their Lord Deputy. Tibóid was to be granted most of the lands of the MacWilliam in Mayo; he would continue as leader of his mother's army and ships and was given enough money to re-stock his lands and feed his people. O'Neill realised how important a strong Chieftain like Grace would be for his war against the Crown. Inter-clan feuding had once more proved to be the weakness of Gaelic unity: it was now every man for himself.

Closing Years

Grace was now in her late sixties, her seafaring days were coming to a close and by now she had handed over control of her lands and ships to Tibóid. O'Neill was finally beaten at the battle of Kindale in 1601. Here, with 3,000 of his fellow countrymen, Tibóid eventually fought with the English against his old enemy, O'Donnell. Many chieftains preferred to fight with their neighbours rather than unite against the English. Grace died in 1603, the same year as Elizabeth. Grace was buried in the little abbey church on Clare Islands out in the Atlantic. Over the centuries Grace's memory has been kept alive in poetry and song, in folklore and legend.

Grace O'Malley's Descendants

Grace's youngest son Tibóid survived the battle of Kindale and returned to County Mayo. He prospered under the new English system that, after the English victory at Kinsale, replaced the Gaelic ancient laws.

In the early years of the 17th century he left his seafaring days behind him, moving inland from Clew Bay to the lands around Lough Mask which was once part of his father's MacWilliam estate. In 1603, he received a knighthood from King James I, the successor of Elizabeth. Tibóid still lived the life of a Gaelic lord rather than an English one. At length he represented Mayo in parliament in Dublin. He held out against the new political and economic system in Connaught and was one of the few Gaelic Lords to have increased their lands under the English monarchy.

At his death he owned 60,000 acres of land, making him the largest landowner in County Mayo. In 1627 he was made First Viscount Mayo by King Charles I. He died in 1629 and was buried in Ballintobber Abbey, County Mayo. He left four sons and three daughters by his wife Maeve O'Connor Sligo. His eldest son Myles succeeded him to the title and much of his estate was divided between his three other sons. There were eight Viscounts before the title died out around the turn of the 19th century.

Today, Grace's descendants live in Westport House, County Mayo, built near the original O'Malley castle of Cathair-na-mar. Grace's other surviving son continued to live at Dunowen Castle in Connemara, dying in 1626 and was buried in the abbey of St Francis in Galway City. Her grandson was dispossessed of his lands by

Oliver Cromwell. His descendants lived on in Connemara for many generations, eventually becoming tenants of their former ancestral lands.

Also from Michael Sheane

The Celtic Supernatural

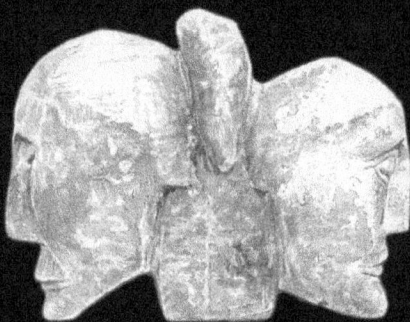

◆ MICHAEL SHEANE ◆

"In the stories connected with Samhain, the Dagda is represented as a grotesque figure of immense strength and appetites. He is clad in the garments of a servant. His weapon is a great club, sometimes dragged on wheels, and he sports a magic cauldron which provides inspiration. The great chalk-cut figure of a naked man wielding a club must represent such a god. The Dagda has been depicted with a hammer and a cup or dish which may be the counterpart of the cauldron."